Dominicanish

ISBN 978-1-882161-37-9 1-882161-37-8

Josefina Báez/Ay Ombe Theatre
P.O.Box 1387
Madison Square Station
New York NY 10159

Dominicanish

Text by Josefina Báez

Photos by Giovanni Savino

Commutative law-Syntax re-routes.
Games.

Every time this text is published is re-organized in a different way; for the fun of it called the multiplicity of meanings and found possibilities.
This is its 8th version.

Dominicanish 8/10

"One of the most important interventions that, to my knowledge reflects on the Dominican cultural experience, we owe it to Josefina Báez, a New York based performer with her work Dominicanish.

Dominicanish offers an open ontological framework where everything that empirically fits in the lives of the Dominican diaspora is part of the identity formation of what we are as a nation, here and there"

"Una de las mas importantes intervenciones que conozco en la reflexión sobre la experiencia cultural dominicana se la debemos a Josefina Báez, la artista 'performera' radicada en Nueva York, en su obra Dominicanish.

Dominicanish ofrece un marco ontológico abierto en donde todo lo que cabe empíricamente en la vida de los compatriotas en la diáspora necesariamente ha de entrar en la formación de lo que somos aquí y allá"

Prof. Silvio Torres Saillant
(Syracuse University)
Desde la orilla: Hacia una nacionalidad sin desalojo

Dominicanish

Dominicanish

El present is a gift.

Full of **morisoñando** con Minute Maid.

Full fridge.

To die dreaming as a maid in a minute.

El present…

Loud colors   On silent faces.

Rude dances   On angels faces.

…**a gift**.

Sounds dancing   Angels facing loud silent.

Silence   On colored faces.

'Who can tell what detours are ahead? *i

Another trial?

Sure.

Another jail?

Maybe.

But if you beat the habit again and kick TV,

no jail on earth can worry you too much.

Tired? You bet. But all that I'll soon forget with my man'.

'But then again, kings and servants depend on each other.*ii

There can be no king without a servant.

And no servant without **a king**.

For silk comes out of **a worm**.

Gold out of rocks. Fire from a piece of wood.

But have you heard of the friendship of **a king**?

As you have heard **a gambler** that is honest.

A snake that forgives   A passionate woman who is calm

An impotent man who is brave

A drunk with discrimination.

But then again, how can servants be well?

It is said that the poor, the sick, the dreamers and the **fools**

always go into exile.

Poor, sick, dreamers and **fools** exile.'

But you see…

There's no guarantee.

Love is like a faucet it turns on and off.

Love is like a faucet it turns on and off.

In off   enough   in off.

There's no guarantee.

Without accent or PhD.

Güiri güiri on dreams.

Even laughing.

Laughing in Dominican**ish**.

There's no guarantee.

Ni aquí ni allá.

Not even with your **güiri güiri** papers.

There's no guarantee.

But first of all, baseball has been very very very good to me.

"Let's be **real**   Let's do the **impossible**".

Take off every safety pin in your way.

Unleash this starched sari.

Let its prints and colors play wild **ragas**.

Foreplaying to the juciest kalankhan.

Foreplaying in the juciest dulce de leche.

'For example you see a rope and think it is a snake. *iii

As soon as you realize that the rope is a rope, your false

perception of a snake stops, and you are no longer

distracted by the fear which it inspired.

Therefore, one who wants to liberate herself must

know the nature **of the** real **self** and the unreal.

When appearances cannot distract you anymore,

then comes knowledge; then comes complete discrimination of

the real and the unreal.

When the vision of reality comes,

the veil of ignorance is completely removed.

When our false perception is corrected, our misery ends.'

Monolingual linear **lover**.

'Julio, te quiero mucho*iv

pero no tanto para morir por ti.

Marisol   tú no entiendes. Tú no me quieres.

Ejmaj, tú nunca me has **querido**.

Marisol   you don't understand   you don't love me

In fact you have never loved me.'

Julio mi amor don't say that, remember what

happened to Anita Rosa Raúl and now

Lourdes in decisiones 1, 2, 3, 4, 5, 6, 7, 8, 9

187   781 718 1 o 2   201   212.

Every sin' is vegetable.

Vegetable   vegetable.

Refrigerator   refrigerator   fridge.

Comfortable com fort able com fortable.

Wednesday   sursdei   zerdeis.

Once in a while.

Everi' sin'

Son sin'   something sin.

Some Son sang **Song** Sin Sing. Sí. **Sing**. Song.

In a cloud of smoke I found my teachers.

In an LP jacket I found my teachers.

Stitched suede   bell bottoms **on**.

Openly displaying their horoscope signs.

Gemini   Capricorn   Pisces   leo lio.

In that cover I found my teachers.

Los hermanos Tonga Isley

Los hermanos Isley.

The Isley Brothers.

"Drifted on a memory*v

ain't no place I'd rather be than with you

yeah   loving you   Well three times

Well well well.

Day will make a way for night.

All I need is a candle light and a song.

Yeah   soft and long   yeah.

Glad could be here alone with a lover unlike no other.

Sad to see a new horizon slowly coming into view   yeah.

I want to be living for the love of you.

Oh yes I am.

All that I'm giving I for the love of you   oh right now."

Very very very very good.

ING the **sweetest** of actions.

And yet… thanks to the Ganga   gracias al Ganjes

los tígeres de Bengala no enchinchan la sed.

El salto del **tígere** hace rato que no es tántrico.

Thanks to the Ganga Bengal Tigers don't move me.

Long gone tantric attacks.

Baseball has been very very very good to me.

I went back there on vacation.

You know better than anybody else how I used to die **to sing**

like Fausto Rey.

There is La Romana.

Here is 107th street ok.

Tú sabes inglés?

Ay habla un chin para nosotros ver si tu sabes.

Forgotten deities

Looked at me   recognized me.

In the process they became

turmeric yellow.

I   jet black.

Bilingual bicultural bacá.

I was changed.

They were changed.

He she it were changed too.

Pretérito pluscuamperfecto.

Indicativo.

imperativo.

Back home   home is 107 ok.

Cool as a cucumber   like Peter thru his house.

Leather leather lederísima.   Tell me with who are you hangin'
out and I will tell you who you are. Por h o por R that doesn't
ring a bell. Out of the woods. Just out of the boat…
with two left feet.

But past is not **present**.

El present is a **gift**.

Boy   Girl loves you   She did   She does   She will.

Chi tu chi sa chi be   chi mu   chi cho   que bien.

A as in Michael.

M as in apple.

La lista crece   La lista creció.

14

Presente y pasado   simple.

Crece creció creciendo.

One way to Santo Domingo.

Exchanged 12.50 Exchanged 27.00 Exchange Today 45.00

Suerte que la 107 **se arrulla con** Pacheco.

Pacheco   tumbao añejo.

Pacheco flauta   Pacheco su nuevo tumbao

El maestro   El artista   Tremendo Caché

compartido en Cruz.

Juntos de nuevo como al detalle.

Tres de Café y dos de **azúcar**.

Although zip coded batey.

Water Con Edison galore.

Aquí también los pantis se tienden

en el baño.

I thought that I would never learn English.

No way I will not put my mouth like that.

No way jamás ni never. No way.

Gosh to pronounce one little phrase one must become another
person with the mouth **all twisted**.

Yo no voy a poner la boca así como un guante.

I want my thunder.

Ajjanta weds Ellora

Nuclear weds Namaste

Mira weds Khrisna

Traffic police   for you   with you   always.

Saraswati travels   Durga travels   Surya travels.

Government approved   officer's mess.

Balaguer leave us the fuck alone.

Leave us alone man.

Leave Me alone.

Special signs.

Signs of specials   donde Roy, Foodurama o el 10 cent

Gimbels o Korbette.

10 for 1.99 and free with purchase.

Pay for it   it's **free**.

Repeat after me   **free**   repeat after you   **free**.

I U   a e o iu you.

Ver very very good.

God bless the child travelin' light.

Sa Ri Ga Ma Pa Da Ni Sa

Home is where theatre is.

DO RE MI FA SOL LA **SI**

Very very very very good to me.

Aquí los discos traen un cancionero.

Discos del alma con afro. Con afro black is beautiful.

Black is a color.

Black is my color.

My cat is **black**.

Repeated a whisper.
Whispered a little louder.
Sing a song.
Sang a song.
Sang **a whisper**.

An' da' si.

Crooked City.

A woman named cupid.

City   glorifying the finest brutality in blue.

City   "nuestro canto con viva emoción. *iv

City   "a la guerra a morir se lanzó. *iv

City   My king of contradictions.

City   That verbal addict.

City   Linear **Lover**.

The list grows   the list grew.

Grows grew growing.

Growing smooth   soft   hard

Growing hard   Sweet memory

Growing soft   Sweet passion.

Growing up   horizon.

Promise everlasting.

Each and every day you are the heaven I need to see.

Every day…

Tour **of** idiomatic expression.

Class **consciousness**.

Fight it   fight it.

Fight it regular   fight it irregular.

Ain't no place I'd rather be than with you.   Yeah.

Loving you   well three times.

Well well well.

You are real   you are constant.

You are the top in **my priority**.

In my priority   you are the top.

In the top   you are my priority.

In my priority   you are the top.

Are you the top in my priority?

Top top **top**   **priority**

Top top top   priority.

A E O
I U.
You.
A mor   And more   Add more.
Mister Juarez, My ESL teacher and later Mrs. Kisinsky, my

monolingual teacher were amazed, 'cause I had the vocabulary found in wet tongues and hookie party goers. And I, believe it or not, was none **of the** above.

Me   the Dominican **miracle** in 84th street.

 In Brandeis representin'.

Writing phrases and sentences in perfect syntax.

Filled and full of sensual images.

Yesterday in homeroom and today in the cafeteria, the bilingual students me cortaron los ojos. They looked at me with the who-you-think-you-are-bitch attitude. And the North Americans laughed at my corny vocabulary.

I ain't no bilingual nerd.

I'm just immersed in the poetry of the senses.

Poetry that leads to acts of love.

Like a prayer.

Like foreplaying.

Dominican cake any occasion.

Repeat after them.

My teachers   the Isley Brothers.

Last Saturday my teachers sang in Soul Train.

Now I don't care how my mouth looks.

I like what I'm saying

Boy   Girl **loves** you   She does   She doesn't

Don't get me wrong   yo se un chin   yo me sé

Girl loves you   Me Tarzan   you Jane

You Me Mine   **love** you do   does   and doesn't
Been very   very very good to me mine myself.

Well   well   well.

A woman named City

Crooked cupid.

City.

Hips swing   male or female.

We swing creating our tale.

Male or female   we swing.

No one to blame or complain but go.

Just go   let go   go slow   go fast.

But go.

Trips to the airport   rest in peace.

Past.

Past perfect   perfect past.

Regular   irregular.

ING very very very good.

Ando cantando.

ING singing.

Di Ar er ir.

Let's go to the house of the Lord

Brujo haitiano.

Brujo Colombiano.

Brujo de **las Matas**.

Frequent flying to the dictionary

Grooving it.

Diggin' it.

Fight the power   fight the power   fight it.

Past is not present.

GED ESL free classes.

GED Free. Free ESL. Classes.

GED ESL Citizenship classes.

Citizenship free. Free GED. ESL free. Classes Free.

Smoke shop 24 hours   calls 39 cents a minute.

Calling cards Arepa to Mangú.

STD ISD PCO STD ISD PCO

Fax   to let   best of both world.

For hire   please sound horn.

Veg. Non-veg.

Hotel.

Fresh tickets.

Alexander the Grape. **Whatchmacallit.**

Repeat after me   Whatchmacallit.

Here I am   chewing English

and spitting Spanish.

Me da vergüenza poner la boca así.

Now I'm another person.

Gu nai

Mouth twisted.

Nai gu.

Higher Education took me to places of pain and pleasure.

History in black and white.

Distinguished teachers: Pearl Bailey, Earth Fantasy,

Wind September, Reasons and Fire.

Ella Fitzgerald, Louis Armstrong.

And the dearest of all, my favorite, Ms. Billie Holiday.

Teaching me the ups and downs of the heart.

The other side of love.

Pero I U   you.

You in a secret   you in a whisper.

Repeat after me   repeat after them.

Repeat after them   repeat after me.

SAT scores doubled but in no university catalog

I found my teachers: The Isley Brothers.

I did not see no class, department, major, minor, sororities,

fraternities, grooving with soul.

No, no, no Samantha, Ronald is the cutest

and then Marvin.

Now I'm part of my teachers' tour.

Smoke and all   **the Garden**

Smoke and all   the Apollo

Smoke and all   the Great Hall in San Francisco

A turn before the guitar solo

Side Side Side   Side Side Side

Point Turn Stop.

Point   Turn   Stop.

Point.

Turn.

Stop.

Poetry taught by my teachers: The Isley Brothers.

Celebrando Abril

Repeat after me.

Celebrando Abril.

Güiri güiri on dreams.

Güiri güiri business.

Here, there, anywhere…

Güiri güiri business.

…very very very very good.

…well well well.

Con el swing del tumbao y reculando como Ciguapa…

Me chulié en el hall.

Metí mano en el rufo.

Craqueo chicle como Shameka Brown.

Hablo como Boricua

y me peino como Morena.

La viejita de abajo no e' viejita ná.

El super se está tirando a la culona del 5to piso.

Jangueo con el pájaro **del barrio**.

Me junto con la muchacha que salió preñá.

Salgo con mi ex.

Hablo con el muchacho que estaba preso.

Garabatié paredes y trenes.

City   I pulled the emergency.

If you want to be prompted in English
press **one**.

If you want to be prompted in Spanish
press **two**.

Enter your card number.

To place a domestic but not a national call
dial 809.

Su llamada no progresó.

Su…no progresó.

Su. No.

No progresó.

Todos los circuitos están cerrados.

Trate su llamada luego   1 Kk.

Please leave your message at the
sound of the beep.

Dominican Cake Any Occasion.

∞

Dominicanish was staged and had a production life of 10 years (November 1999-November 2009); directed by Claudio Mir. The last performances were held at Harlem Stage NYC. Giovanni Savino photographs, shared here, are from the last performance (November 8th, 2009).

Special thanks to each and every one part of this journey called Dominicanish. Om Is.

Josefina Báez (La Romana, Dominican Republic/New York). Storyteller, performer, writer, theatre director, educator, devotee. Founder and director of Ay Ombe Theatre (1986). Alchemist of creative life process: Performance Autology (creative process based on the autobiography and wellness of the doer). Books published: Dominicanish (publish in 10 versions), Comrade, Bliss ain't playing, Dramaturgia I & II, Como la una/Como uma, Levente no. Yolayorkdominicanyork, De levente. 4 textos para teatro performance, Canto de plenitud, Latin In (Antología de Autología), As Is E' (anthology) and Why is my name Marysol? (a children's book).

Josefina Báez (La Romana, República Dominicana/Nueva York). ArteSana, cuenta cuentos, performera, escritora, directora de teatro, devota. Fundadora y directora de Ay Ombe Theatre (abril 1986). Alquimista del proceso para vida creativa: Autología del Performance (proceso creativo basado en la autobiografía y bienestar del hacedor/a). Libros publicados: Dominicanish (ha ser publicado en 10 diferentes versiones), Comrade, Bliss ain't playing, Dramaturgia I & II, Como la una/Como uma, Levente no.Yolayork dominicanyork, De Levente. 4 textos para teatro performance, Canto de Plenitud, Latin In (antología de autología), As Is E' (textos reunidos) y ¿Por qué mi nombre es Marysol? (cuento para niños y niñas).

www.josefinabaez.com

Gratitude galore to Giovanni Savino.
Our fruitful co-creations are filled and full of joy as we surf the As Is ever changing –el na', el to'.

Giovanni Savino. New York City based photographer specialized in editorial, documentary and portrait. His work themes are various and all have that closeness to our guts and hearts; his books frame life –raw and exquisite-as closest as it can get.

www.giovannisavinophotography.com

Cited sources

i* From The Essential Billie Holiday. Carnegie Hall Concert. #13. Narration. Verve.

ii* Vishnu Sharma, Panchatantra. India. Text edited to suit Dominicanish.

iii Shankara Adi. Viveka Chudamani. India. Text edited to suit Dominicanish.

iv from a public ad sponsored by the NYC Health Department. AIDS subway campaign 1990.

v Lyrics of song produced, written, arranged and composed by The Isley Brothers and Chris Jasper (For the Love of you).

vi From the Dominican Republic's National anthem.

Vii From the Dominican Republic's National anthem.

Ay Ombe
Theatre

Made in the USA
Columbia, SC
18 August 2021